without title

Other works by Gerry Loose include

Change (images by K. Sweeney McGee)
Yuga Night (with Larry Butler & Kathleen McGee)
Knockariddera
a measure
Eitgal
Being Time
The Elementary Particles
Tongues of Stone
Printed on Water — New & Selected Poems *
Ten Seasons
the deer path to my door
that person himself *
fault line
An Oakwoods Almanac *
Night Exposures
The Great Book of the Woods
Twelve Airs

as editor

The Holistic Handbook
Seed Catalogue (with Morven Gregor)
Ten Seasons: explorations in botanics
        (with photographs by Morven Gregor)

as editor & translator

The Botanical Basho (with Yushin Toda)
Mither Tongue (translations of Jidi Majia's poetry into Scots)

*Shearsman titles

without title

Gerry Loose

Shearsman Books

First published in the United Kingdom in 2024 by
Shearsman Books
P.O. Box 4239
Swindon
SN3 9FN

Shearsman Books Ltd Registered Office
30–31 St. James Place, Mangotsfield, Bristol BS16 9JB
(this address not for correspondence)

www.shearsman.com

ISBN 978-1-84861-866-4

Copyright © Gerry Loose, 2024

The right of Gerry Loose to be identified as the author of this work has been asserted by him in accordance with the Copyrights, Designs and Patents Act of 1988.
All rights reserved.

Contents

impromptu poem at Bac Giang, Vietnam	7
littoral rising	8
Weather Mountain	12
will your mouth kiss carnations	14
summer in Montpellier, the Botanic Garden	16
in praise of nothing	40
on home ground	41
Bodhisattvas of Medellín	43
in which	44
let's talk about trees	55
walking in, walking on	57
under the tarmac the garden	65
the corners of the seasons	67
what breaks	69
light split dew	70
we breathe	71
notes towards a Pavilion for Listening to Rain	72
old invective directive against autumn poems	80
the deer path to my door	81
airs	93
guilt is a partial truth	100
folly	101
the grounds	104
without title	107
acknowledgements	131

for Morven Gregor

impromptu poem at Bac Giang, Vietnam

for Morven, as ever

here is the flower
I could not pick

I left it for the branch
I left it for the bee I saw

& now
here it is for you

*****

littoral rising

1
after Amergin

am glacier rolling back
am tsunami
am beaching whale
am the bones of every curlew
am stag starving on hill
am hawk down to bone
am wilt of green plant
am ribcage hind
am salmon infested with lice
am the end of words
am burning teardrop
am salt ocean in woodland
am plastic in every pore
am head burst with fire

who gouges & grubs blue mountains
who trudges the crescent moon
who stores suns in buried bunkers
who leaches the fecund topsoils
whose alibi is god
who stands at the edge
who holds back the typhoon

2

Thalassa Thalassa
how littoral slides into us
edge become centre

coffin sea-road
a gesture of longshore drift
of foreshore & nearshore

how the oceans rise in them
& they clamp shells to ears
to contain surf

sweet sap rises in them
to restrain salt from eyes

barnacles & men of war
in upper branches
their canopies bird wings

the strand become charnel
the eyes' restless waves

deep tribes of swimfish
as architecture of water

nippled porpoises
as sea-surge of wheatfield

that slow mountain wave
that slow mountain swimming

& how sky holds up the waters
& the oceans roost in trees

& islands disappear
in salt

3

after psalm 74

Oh man, why does your anger burn with acrid smoke?
Why do your tramplings deliver perpetual desolations?
How should you be rewarded for clear-felling each ancient forest?
What is the price of breaking the five wild oceans?
What are your terrible secrets spoken in the mouth of Leviathan?
Where now is the stolen soul of the turtle dove?
Oh man, stand up: plead your own cause

4

after nothing
as lines are drawn

for the sea
so for the coast

as docken rusts
so the burnet rose

stem by stem purple
foxgloves reach higher

yellow mustard
& yellow crusts of lichen

singing pink thrift
woodbine surging

pignut & cow parsley
drift on drift in June sun

whitecaps of elder froth
winged rust of sycamore seed

so are we
it is

as grace loaned

Weather Mountain, Noboribetsu, Hokkaido

for Morven

sediments and breccias
striated and baked
this is north

the cold caldera at once
erupting filling Jigokudani
Hell Valley with its hell

it can only be done by walking
it concerns walking
it's here we walk away from & to

the same place

what's true of mountains?

their stone hearts are magma

we plant trees
that mountains can walk again
that mountains can shrug them off & sleep
(they are full of demons when wakened)

what do I know of mountains?

I know I'm walking

we plant trees
that I can walk
big toe divided

that's the way it's done here

the mountain breathes through fumitories
on snow & ice
(breath frosting)
where hell's inventors
boil believers of another hell

where do the bears sleep?
where do the boars walk?
snow is dreaming our footprints

crane dancing
basket headed musicians
inventing only ourselves

what is the yeast of hell?
Weather Mountain
what is being stolen?
Hiyori yama

the language of the body
is weather
the dialect of sulphur is restless here

side booth demons stink of it
Weather Mountain walks its own temple
Weather Mountain its own ringing bell

will your mouth kiss carnations
(Pablo Neruda)

for Morven

we know that nothing is given
& everything is received

& with empty hands every
thing is given so

every thing is an answer
everything un answered

so empty hands holding
from then for now for then

bitter lemons' yellow
watered with dew

a weight of quinces
through rooms and chambers

an oozing of plums
with the lancings of wasps

oh the embracing of redness
from vines and from vinehouse

tearful pears
along cheek and chin

a lapsang of camellia tea
with waves of the firth

& pomes and more apple
each more apple than before

in blue air impersonating
mountain shimmering

& the rose & the rose rose
hips & mouths kissing

& from then for now for
then when you kiss

& know that all is received
& everything is ludic

summer in Montpellier, the Botanic Garden

1

patois tumbling Occitan, Latin, Arabic, Hebrew
Muslim, Jew, Cathar, Christian

left a wingbeat in the sky to return to later:

cicadas chirring in their dialect

a sign, Jupiter becoming Saturn perennial becoming bush

liquidambar

black ants foraging for red blood

noonday sleepers on benches of dust & stone

two gardeners, hands on hips under the only unlabelled tree after searching patiently for an hour for seedlings

raked path edges which tell of markings of desert scriptures of distant sutras

some dozens of hundreds of the fruit of the mulberry Morvus alba which fall are falling taken only by birds

those same mechanic cicadas whirring lower than shrilling jinking soaring coasting wheeling swallows

the bell tolling sixty seven times at seven in the evening

wandering the length of the flâneur twilight

2

hills, the long purple evening hills
& into darklit Theatre of Anatomy
what we should not see they say
dark closed-room aborted secrets
cut apart, torn, ripped from life
palpitating, flayed, stripped from ourselves
to ease apart the skin
to pull apart skin
to ease over the muscle
to send the knife where it will
to count throbbing organs
& the chambers of the lungs

moon bitten eaten cancered by clouds
shrivelled pain held in alcohol
in aspic blinded in vitriol in glass

the light then the lights of a distant town
the pine in Gerhard Street which enjoys
singing its cicadas

3

there are many reckonings
I counted them
she is on a bicycle with eleven parrots
she is on a scooter with two dogs running
she is on a stone stair with a lizard

she is alone with how many hands
what does she hold

open the light

4

as Garden Directors become bitter
jealous, then stone:
Rondelet, blind
Pelissier, priest, blind
Belleval, debtor, blind
Sauvages, blind
Dunal from a distance appears to see
spiders in Granel's sockets
Galavielle with webs & pine needles in his
Martins, empty sockets
Planchon, eyeless

5

it is forbidden

              among other things
              speech

we listen carefully
heed little among tongues

the grass
is forbidden

				poetry
				is a kind of music

you must hear it in
order to judge

6

in the nothing
in the unclear mind
in the going & coming
of water lit sun
shafts under trees

7

what can be
brought from here

a thousand seeds
a thousand words

a thousand arms
of compassion

peace, cicada
peace

8

rooted in perfection

lotus   maple   osage

& the Judas tree
unassailable perhaps

9

a twentieth century story
of noble birth
surviving revolution
fleeing war
though not wealth
resorts to painting
what's abstract to you
Zao says
is real to me

an old tortoise
finally in mud
what he likes best
next to painting
is to smile

10

mouth full of stones
olives of the region
cherries of the region
fill my mouth with songs
with song leaves

11

the music
& here's the diamond
the heart
drops of water
beads of water
pearls of water
stones of water
tears of water
blood of water here

the fountain's turned off at six in the evening
there, it is kept turned off

12

shadows
traced in sand
& bells pealing

fading

13

yarrow
tansy
poppies
plantain
sow thistle
arnica
knotweed
all-heal

14

the trees, once human
Bacchus, Jupiter, once divine
become bitter, jealous
toes thrust into myth & story
become paper & word
written

Thracian women see
cracked wood spreading
along their soft thighs
root as Oak

a foul mouthed shepherd's voice
-box grown rigid, gnarled
what's left of his tongue
become Olive

the Sungod's daughters
tearing hair for a dead brother
tear Poplar leaves
poplar bark closing over last amber words

to be remembered
when seeds & leaves fall
into my lap &
stick in my hair
where doves come to sip

where fingers
reach down into soil
hair become willow
Rabbi Dov Lior, bitter
jealous: a thousand non-Jewish

lives're not worth
a Jew's fingernails

15

under the swallows
beside the garden

is the tramcar
direct to Odyssey

16

not a new game, destruction
what's in a name, Valéry?
a garden of epithets
a dictionary garden
what do they not see
no independent arising
our garden is whose desert?

what's in a name,
Rondelet, Pelissier, Belleval?
between tongues
a dictionary falls from lips
a self-naming
a transhumance of people
refugee
after their own horti
culture
drawn on Tassili dune caves

Sauvages
what shall we say to Lior
to Saïd   to Yousef
to Lbou   to Hassan
Chani, Abdelhak & Tibou?

In another room
a man sings
softly *oh oh*
eh eh tomorrow
eh eh tomorrow
& falls asleep

a jet passes overhead.

17

something like history slips in
dogs bark & drop delicate turds in the street
virtuoso musicians & jazzmen
strike up in squares where
we dine on terraces

something like war elsewhere

in another room she sobs
she sobs, heart become pebbles
her sleep will turn mosquitoes
into droning planes

18

the whole of July

doing what
a taxonomy of reality
recognition before thought

yesterday's flower is
no more
is to see the impermanent

as permanent
mind traces   today in flower
unnoticed before

delicate white
starry jasmine
Trachelospermum jasminoides

white pink apricot red
oleander
Nerium oleander

recognised not described
lotus
Nelumbo

today the cicadas
are reborn as cicadas
their old skins abandoned

lives walked away from
on tree trunks
the cicadas

are climbing out
of what
they would not recognise

19

he sings of his hidden house
in the lemon orchard

I also have a little house in a garden
just for the present

I talk to cicadas
& the fish in bubbling water

also talk of love
among these flowers

20

in another street he sings
I'm chocolate, chocolate that's me

our frailty as people walking
our oddity dreaming

those who sleep soundly
are the jailers of the street

21

our aim to wake
another going round
we'll grow a revolution
we'll grow our own tongues
a lilting an utterance
sage & rue
whole vocabularies
of grapes on the vine
each fig's a proverb
each mulberry a lyric
red tomatoes small sweet nothings
a thesaurus of cherries whispering

names cannot be sold
only given & received

*

it is July 14th in this
Year of Grace

he sits in the street
singing still   softly

his feet are carefully
folded

into old soiled rags

*

Raimon d'Avinhon
caustic *trobador*:
a servant
meat porter & hijacker
ruffian & trafficker
fisherman & horseman
friend of streetgirls
thief & rat catcher
stonemason drunkard
baker & writer
milliner & grocer
maker of weapons of war
swine herd
bin raker
fool to those who believe it
sage to them as find him so
a good physician
when it's time

Did we walk the streets alone
ranting loudly each to himself
anger at our livers

Did we play Roma violins for cigarettes & coins
& abuse

we know *oud* was played
in the Theatre of Anatomy
& gargoyles of the old cloister gaped
& we briefly applauded the

divine in music under a new moon
shining on the west rondel of the Cathedral

    & the stars   the stars.

Why is peace forbidden?

       Did one of us walk seventy feet up
along the aqueduct ledge
     gesturing, muttering, throwing
down random wild flowers – weeds
       upturned faces at pavement cafes
a pause in *Midi Libre*
       not wanting to jump
but there anyway

Did another sit patient, begging
in that square
dedicated to the Martyrs of the Resistance
pennies in an ashtray
marked *3 centuries*

22

wintersweet
sorrel
equisetum
daisy
dandelion, that piss-a-bed
sedums
ferns
simples for cures

what simple for cloudwalking
on aqueducts

sweet winter rains
now's the time

*

migrating
coming & going

better
to listen than talk

what
is a state of mind

leaning
back in the chair

soles
& heels flat against a cool wall

shrilling
of cicadas striking hot stone

grove's
interiors

shapeless
shapely the mind learns to walk

shadows
of bars on the insides of eyes

23

dust
      & the very planes of light

what
> is a state of mind

tight
> right into the heart (it moves)

&
> gone with the dappling leaves

green
> chambers of sunlight

24

garden riddles

who stole the stars
& dropped them in the dust?
jasmine

who stole the sun
& gave us each a piece?
the orange

who stole the rain
& sent it straight up again?
bamboo

who stole water
& turned it to wine?
the grape

who stole time
& sent it spiralling?
snail

who stole our labour
& turned it to gold?
the king

who stole the gold
& gave it liquid flesh?
koi carp

who stole the fattest carp
from the king's garden?
the hanged man

25

at night
back from sleep

I ask droning mosquitoes
to bite me

leave alone
flesh of the one I hold

26

I've counted the measure
of the plane leaf in fives

each not one but
not in its own tongue

it wasn't rain but
pattering of zelkova

seed & green distressed
by wind & heat

size of raindrops
dusting the place of trees

*

to consider form
the whole long leaf

lit afternoon
considering seeds

*

to consider time
the cicadas chirred

three times a second
for endless minutes

on edge
magpies at counterpoint

*

clapping game of a mother
with her daughter

syncopation of water
striking bamboo

& reddening
pod by pod day by

day along the month
of Italian lilies

to send a blaze
through woodland floor

27

one noon in another
room in open air

with a handful of
hot radishes, some bread

cracking almonds, drinking
wine dregs,

in the mouth of
Arnaut Daniel

il miglior fabbro
Occitan:

it's better made
in mother tongue

& the alouette
cackled at that

28

eyes dance with leaf
the other side of veins

petulant, the sun king points
to clouds once more

with moon
beyond his reach

29

one two three four
five six seven & eight times

shadow of moving water
shade of a singing voice

sleep is the bridge
to mother tongue

30

herder of hills
little runner of waters

what is emptiness

Roch, in the seventeenth

year of his age, not yet a saint
set out on pilgrimage

to a place older than God
older than that grove

at the source of the Verdus
where Diana bathed

(& for setting eyes on her
turned another to a stag

torn apart by his own hounds)
& simply helped

pustulent sufferers
of the black death.

Roch, no spring in his step
but autumn revealed

the way he took
the road which walks itself

31

here water leaps
toward frog kingdoms

ponds swallow
with a smack of lips

in a republic of water
all princes end

their days squatting
under the meniscus

jumping at
every common footfall

32

plant misery
harvest anger

heart of a heart
in the old city
a garden
in the old garden
an old tree
its old trunk grown in
& clasping itself
writhing with a hundred eyes
& gargoyling wooden mouths
arthritic mother's skin
stretched luminous over bone

in old mouths
wishes are posted
paper scraps

I have need of money

I hope to be serene
for the health of my family
I want a job
that my sisters stay happy as I left them
love & prosperity to the end

Diderot, I hope our story continues

peace in Israel
peace in Palestine
peace in Iraq

who thanks the tree
with leaves of tongue

in the old garden
in the old city

that those I made suffer
may forgive

the practice of compassion
compassion

33

holly-leaved oak
mulberry with plane leaves
tansy-leaved phacelia
whole-leaved jaborose
lamb-leaf Tartary

maple with leaves of ash

34

to sit where
the salamander sage

creeps out for sun
sage of the Himalayas

sage of the Nile
sage of Iranian mountains

sage of Turkestan
sage of the woods

sage of the boreal
morning

35

remember that first night
you left before dawn

here in the shade of trees

in praise of nothing

in your house there should be nothing
your house should be nothing but a hut, a shelter

in your hut there should be
three shelves, which is all you need

the first is for books you cannot remember
the second is for herbs and pulses
the third is pots, pans and knives

the second shelf is highest
since though you are happy to share with mice
rice and your sheltering books are forbidden

there will also be a fire or
these days an iron stove, surrounded by logs

nothing but logs and kindling
you have gathered, felled and split
with your own axe and nothing hands

maybe your nothing also
contains a bucket and cup for nebulous water

you understand
you have something of nothing
which is everything

on home ground

on not meeting Du Fu in Skeoch Wood
twelve hundred and fifty one years after he left

    each day the paths grow deeper in leaves no-one here
    the hound runs there & here back to check on me
    I think like father & son we love each other
    the jays scold us for walking on acorns
    maple leaves keep falling tree limbs cracking
    for a few days no duties tonight I'll drink more wine
    who needs me sober ravens fly upside down

*

    pandemic & storms two years
    away from the hut heart failed half
    blind in one eye fearful for the other

    woods and hills walk on
    leave me here reading Du Fu
    dreaming of the orchard

    flyting owls flying geese
    I'll steal the stars set them anew
    such freedom in staying still

*

notes on flying

    though they walk polite
    dogs here these days

    the hound & I stravaig
    the woods' upper reaches

together we almost soar
he bounds for sheer joy

heart dancing left footed
grey haired stumbling

after even myself
flying into emptiness

Bodhisattvas of Medellín

The fliers for massage parlours, two-for-one pizzas, bars, the losing lottery tickets, condoms, sweetie wrappers, empty cigarette packets, the minotaurs and the nymphs; the angels: the street sweeper collects, files and labels them all. He sweeps and waits. Tomorrow there will be more.

In 54th Street, Caracas, at dusk, from the deep hole in the ground lined with wood, ascending the steel ladder left in place, they arrive: one, two, three & four & a fifth, tired, but they arrive.

Oh the laughter of the women of the house clearing dishes after the guests have gone to bed! Oh their tears! Oh their beards!

In the place of guns, she, her with dyed hair, lets off fire-crackers & laughs too.

The flower seller has arranged the lilies. He rests on his broom. He is tired of sweeping decaying sentient beings.

& the one who sells aphrodisiac ants from a small tray.

Bodhisattvas of Medellín, walking on & walking through, I took a photograph of your heart.

in which

He's ninety five, the shepherd. He has two dogs, one old, one young, both circling him. He walks the pasture, one elbow crutch, one stick. He talks about the wind, while scanning all around for his last lambing ewe, gone missing. Possibly the young heifers, newly released in the pasture, have kicked up and knocked the lamb. How humbly he owns the sky. In his arm gesture, with the south wind, is the western paradise.

The man of the Tower is angry. He knows what it's all about. I know what this is about he shouts. I know what this is all about; it will never happen. He emphasises: It will never happen. Above the Tower, cirrus clouds.

There are many necessary stones, the Minister thinks. She tries to resist the impulse to walk with hands behind her back, left hand round right wrist. I should give these as presents she thinks. Who understands the giving of a stone? In the distance, along the strand, the rocks have taken the shape of people. Realization, slow in coming, is that we are strangers everywhere, every step.

The arborist sits on an upturned traffic cone, looking up into the tree. She lights a cigarette.

The hound and the one who does nothing walk a clear half mile right at the water's edge on an incoming tide, knowing that the sea will erase their tracks. Only their shadows remain in the morning sun, leaving the littoral pristine, to be discovered by those who might come later. The bull seal saw them pass.

In which seals turn into smooth great grey boulders. Long after the ferry has passed the bow wave reaches the shore. The shore, the Minister is thinking, is a line taking the island for a walk.

Liquidambar trees. The stranded linked floats both read Nordic Fulmar OB81 Ashleigh Jane.

The hound is apprehensive of the ocean and chitters at the musical repetitions and accretions of curl, undertow, roil, boom and suck of surf as it breaks. The corpse of a guillemot, wings folded into the wrack, does not reassure him. For him, nothing is inanimate.

The shepherd, his two sticks, his two dogs, the ewes, lambs: all still, leaning into wind, caught. The aperture closes.

On the low island to the south-east a turbine farms wind, sails turning equinox, pushing cumulus and nimbus. The Minister sits on sea-worn geology at tide's limit between wreckage of two eroded windblown beeches, where razorfish shells gather. The ocean surges. There are no epiphanies except in the oracles of razor and beech, wind and ocean.

Old man gulls chuckling to themselves and cracking mussels. The hare sits on the strand looking out over the calm ocean. Seals manoeuvre onto rocks and peer inland. Small stones have green beards of those luminous weeds of the shallows. The hound buries a jackdaw corpse with his nose. Oystercatchers probe silence with their wheeling songs.

Oh, the white flesh of Magnolia dealbata petals. For a brief moment the Minister does not grind her teeth.

This day after many grey days the shepherd welcomes back his shadow. The Minister has her nose down on the beach, picking up small yellow shells. The shepherd slowly passes along the pasture immediately above the beach; he notes the Minister. She does not see him pass. The Minister has never met the shepherd. He has heard much about her. A warship glides past, grey against the greying mainland coastline.

He can drive just fine, of course, the shepherd. At least in his old white van between the woods and the shoreline where in spring he keeps his three tups and his yearling calves. The voices come from the rock.

The shepherd eyes the dead kid, small as a lamb, soft hooved, long legs. He regards the hind's hoof hollows around the puddle in which the kid lies. A mother's desolation maybe. The kid has no eyes. Nearby four huge felled tree trunks smoulder, partly burned and blackened. Ash under them pink, ochre and fine. Scorched earth. A young hare jinks side to side along the rutted path. There is revelation, he thinks, at the beginning of things rather than their endings. The shepherd empties out his heart. It's the practice of the tides.

The dunlin's cry pierces more than the air as the Minister walks the shingle. The bird is flying ahead and landing almost within reach, a decoy, away from the Minister's steps near the nest. She stoops and picks up a pilgrim's scallop to which the day is riveted. There are sea plants and so many hoppers living inside the bleached horse skull among the shells and shingle. She absently pockets the shell, wayfaring. She is thinking that tears of joy should flow more freely than tears of anger.

And the clouds that became mountains.

The man of the Tower has no focus for his continuing anger. It's directed indiscriminately, explosively. It consumes his gut; it gripes his bladder. There is a bolus, a little stone in his sternum. His misanthropy includes himself. He wishes he hadn't. He wishes he didn't. He wishes he wasn't.

In a half acre field at the place of the ash trees, hard by the Cruel Quarter, the shepherd keeps a handful of small hardy black sheep. He sells the wool. There is no one left who cards and spins, though there is a spinning wheel in the island shop.

In the diminutive gothic church, mind wandering, the arborist notices, not for the first time, the currach behind Columba, who is preaching to the Picts. His hair is lank; he raises a cross high. The helmeted Picts look on, arms folded or leaning on swords and spears. The pulpit, reached by four curving stone steps, is carved with grapes and writhing vines. Below the pulpit is a branch: a prayer tree, with two prayer requests. The arborist categorises: ash; Fraxinus excelsior. Who has gone highest, she thinks, for I would go higher.

The one who does nothing has a name for all the rocks along the strand. Seal rock. Gannet rock. Heron rock. Wrack. Frog rock. The rocks have no name for him, though he passes every day. In today's heavy rain his old waterproof leaks at the shoulders and drips onto his trousers; his pockets are bulging with windfall apples from the tended but unharvested orchard he walks through on the way to the long strand.

The ferryman, who is called after the place he belongs to, suffered ulcers on his legs for many years, though he never complained. He was of the last generation from the island who had some Gaelic. He walked his collie dog every day despite his legs and always said the dog had two spokes. That is, the English and the Gaelic.

Mother would answer the front door to anyone knocking, but when a caller asked could not remember her address. She had a wee smile when the boys – we call them the boys, but they are grown men – lost the paper with the bank details. She told them she knew and zimmer-framed straight to the dresser drawer and pulled it out. The boys can't get over that.

Out of season, to keep her eye in, the mushroom hunter gathers stones from the long strand. They must be of red sandstone, with a stripe of igneous white running through and easily carried in a shoulder bag, like mushrooms, unseen. She unloads the bag in her small garden. After all these years, she sometimes thinks there are more stones than herbs in her garden. She thinks the stones, though, may be medicinal as well as the herbs. She does not count the acanthus.

Today the air is loud with the music of an incalculable number of bees. Running full pelt the hound is not aware of his own grace and beauty. Shine on, forever shine.

Almost without thinking the one who does nothing goes out and buys a half bottle of vodka, that being the cheapest option. He shares it with the bird who breaks the evening silence and where were they before the world began?

Such insistence on laughter from the herring gulls. Two pilots for the passing warship through the reefs. The ferryman narrows his eyes, looks inland.

Seven tears may be shed into the sea. Today, again, the seals are on the rocks, all looking inland because that is where danger comes from. They are, after all, selkies. The hares are sat on their haunches, in a dwam, staring out to the gently rolling sea, where all mysteries come from.

The one who does nothing rarely goes home without something in his pockets or bag: pine cones for kindling, a couple of knuckles from a newly felled pine for the fire, a herb root, kelp for the garden, the patterns of rain squalls on the sea or the hammer of a yaffle. He keeps his hat for mushrooms. He avoids all the others, the way on his bicycle, he once veered around frogs and other smaller beings on his path.

He's liberated at last, the shepherd. His elbow crutch returned to the surgery, he walks a little more freely, though the memory of the body tells him to tread warily still.

Because she walks looking up, to see the canopy and the health of the tree crowns, especially ash, the arborist is always stumbling on stumps and roots. She has developed a slow walk, which enables her to feel her way mostly with her feet, though her boots are heavy.

His head tilted, the shepherd's cap sits crooked. He's amazed by the Perseids.

The Minister would like to ride the island thermals but she has no wings. How often she has enjoyed that cool breeze through the window when sleep is near and the book has been laid aside, reading glasses taken off and the bridge of her nose pinched. Sleep is another dwelling where she meets her dead who are gentle and remote: she can speak with them. Where she sews her left foot back on.

The deer are in no rush. They amble a quarter mile length of the long strand, ears relaxed, enjoying the early morning sun lifting night's chill. Shade in their foot hollows in the shell strewn sand.

The cottage is empty. The shepherd's old coat hangs from a peg in the small open fronted porch. Only the doves are softly talking.

In which autumn dried grasses' long seed heads become roe deer flanks.

Here, the arborist knows, more than anywhere, she is seconds from oblivion. She spreads the roots and carefully plants out a small mint plant from the flower and produce show in town, then weeds around the sapling oaks.

In which a rain sodden fallen trunk, limbless now, still leaning against another living tree, reposes in its decay, and becomes the hound.

Running fresh water the hound can manage: there is a constancy. But sea's waves, he is convinced, are more than the pull of moon on ocean: they are sentient.

And in which an avenue of limes leading down to the sea becomes a nave.

Some days there are shades. That's when the small creel boats become shells. The one who does nothing rejected the rope washed onshore, even though it was thirty feet long and blue. Blue rope, blue seas hidden under cumulus grey. He never goes to the strand without a bow saw and sack.

In the birch woods just the tang and dangle of scarlet rowan berries. The Minister is unsure of colours. How would you call that except that it illuminates the cryptic coloration of autumn in animal mossy birches. On a silent early morning it becomes the light we are all made from.

In which fallen field maple leaves on the path become yellow frogs. On the equinox the one who does nothing pockets fallen horse chestnuts from along that path. There is no-one to give them to. He watches yellow wagtails by the shallow burn. He is glad he has wheat flour for making bread; he's heard the hunger stories of chestnut bread and acorn flour.

The rough paddock sometimes has a horse in it. Bounding the small woodland overlooking the bay, the hound knows every tree. This is his first nose to nose encounter with the horse. It's the first creature he's seen in his young life who is bigger than him. Gently, horse and hound kiss, an ear flicks first in the one, then the other. The hound, with his compassionate soft eyes, acknowledges an ancient bond, passes on.

A mirror in a mirror. Place makes us, the Minister is thinking. A starred cosmos of microfauna and flora under her feet. A jubilance of utterance from all around her – ocean to leaf fall – wave upon wave through her.

The black sheep are hefted, the shepherd has made sure of that. He does not enter them into the agricultural show competitions. Their place is the Quarter they know. He will not display his companions for a rosette.

The man of the Tower has inherited all the archaeology of dissatisfaction from the Tower, which was once the town museum. He is pinned, dessicating, as surely as the butterflies once there in cases.

Leaves are falling and with them unripe chestnuts. From among trees the arborist looks out to sea to note the submarine's conning tower passing out to deep Atlantic, soundwaves booming from the escorts. She looks down. Whatever the season there's a dew-stuck leaf on her left toecap. Dew is all the spiders have caught this morning.

Invigorated by the western gale, the Minister wonders who could possibly doubt that trees talk. Her thoughts are blown leaves. Secretly, she had always wanted to be a rabbi. But the Talmud felt too rigid, a wisdom of the distant past. Instead she studies the esoterica of natural phenomena, rooted in the present: how ants communicate; the dialects of trees.

The warmth of the south westerly brings soft rain. From long experience and, by now, intuition, the mushroom hunter knows to look for hedgehog mushrooms in the place at the wood edge where they grow. They are there of course, having communicated their presence through unseen mycelium, diaphanous threads through the lower sky, just like any fabricated constellation.

We are the raw materials of our dreams, the arborist is thinking. No need to collect red stars or the hard round fruits of the Chilean hazelnut.

In harvested dusk, the pearls of the new birch polypores, the carmine of rowan berries are monastic illuminations in woodland margins. The mushroom hunter's path is lit with delight.

Brushing spiders' lines from his face, seeing movements from the corners of his eyes, thinking fragments of half remembered songs, the one who does nothing steps carefully along his hangover. There's a cool spit of rain, but he keeps his head uncovered, relishing the freshness the rain brings. He's reached the wood edge and the song fragment "said he'd make a new living off of bundling sticks" when the honey fungus horde appears, climbing the full length of the old birch. Although it's a dangerous parasite on trees, he'd not tell the arborist, and certainly not the mushroom hunter. This would settle his head and stomach, he's thinking, with a duck egg from the farm of the portage. He fills his hat with the savoury mushrooms, returned to the here and now.

Geophony. What is the waves' recitation other than the voice of zephyr and moon. It speaks of constellations and their pattern is the lonely songs of porpoises. The mushroom hunter shakes her head from this dwam where she sits on a boulder at the shoreline. She knows where the ceps are waiting for her.

In his pocket the one who does nothing has a serpentine pebble, one of Columcille's tears, as a talisman against drowning, together with a piece of broken blue and white china with a picture of a junk. The blacksmith has work on the mainland and rather than take four hours driving round via the ferry and the meandering coast road has found himself a boat and crosses the channels every day with his men. The one who does nothing'd gone along once, not to visit the Bald Headland across the sea, west, but to see the island from the south, offshore, and the small island of the little saint. He drinks tea while the smith works but does not go ashore there at Crooked Mouth.

The ferry company calendar is on every kitchen wall. With a sense of anticipation, if not something approaching harm-joy, the man of the Tower notes well that it is Friday the 13th. His mouth curves upwards a little as he eyes the blackening clouds to the south west. The arborist decides to leave her chainsaw in the workshop. The Minister strides out, no faltering. Two old men, each with a dog and a stick meet and pass along the path in the whitethorn wood.

In which a bicycle becomes a burn. The glim of beechwoods.

With the sound of the wind always. The arborist surveys her trees in the tail of the hurricane. They are leafless but upright. The union flag on its lonely pole is shredded. The arborist smiles.

In which routine becomes governed by ritual. In which dwelling ends. All bones are the same colour. The light of the quagmire is quenched. The man of the Tower becomes his father; that which he most despises. In which container ships contain nothing.

In which the hound discovers his own two-day-old tracks on the strand and is mazed.

The man of the Tower is not sleeping. From the Tower window where he stands looking out over wine dark sea and sky he is startled by a shooting star. A Leonid meteorite. Debris. Dust. Auguries. He is not heartened.

It's low tide, the day of the Faithful Departed. The cockle picker has finished his morning's work. There used to be forty tons a week, easily picked; now it's barely one ton. His brother is now too old to work, so the cockle picker works for both of them. All the cockles and winkles go to France. One afternoon, he took his mother to the next island and at seventy she picked two hundredweight they were so plentiful, but she never went back. I like to pick them one at a time, she told him. He works in the old measures. He remembers the religious killings on his father's island. He'd burn all the churches if he could.

In which ten thousand beech leaves blown to the strand rise and become one hind. In which brown pebbles become melodious wrens. The centre holds.

The Minister looks across to the bigger island where the Windy Mountain is mountainously walking time. Walking wind. There's quietude and quiet vitality. No passive acceptance, only deep knowledge, she's thinking.

The one who does nothing is wondering what a jay is other than part digested acorn, aerial, rebuking. He can feel the blood behind his eyes.

In which the lip of a wavelet becomes a dunlin. A gable end becomes a red autumn maple.

A small riff of wind on seaswell becomes a kraken. Oarweed rafts reach far into the woodlands. In which the Minister becomes her grandmother. Blue light is scattered. Remembrance of hurricanes brings sand and smoke particles from other continents. A woman's voice becomes a bird. Trees become awakened. Whalsa Lass and Shepherd Lass share morning's moorings.

In which oak becomes strake, quern of the ocean.

let's talk about trees

> Even when you take to the woods,
> you're taking political steps
> on political grounds
> —Wisława Szymborska

There are gods they say and there are trees and there are poets.

A river god turned a water nymph into a laurel tree but her heart
continued beating within, though her hair became leaves, her legs rooted
a thunder god transformed seven sisters to poplars; they still stand by the river
a god of love and beauty folded a woman into a myrrh tree; her tears
        become resin
a god of fruitful earth, castrated, became a pine tree, a plague god with a bow
transfigured a boy into a cypress, his tears, again, flowing as sap. So many tears.

An exiled poet, Ovid, caught between Republic and Empire, his love all sung
calls the gods to mind and makes coded songs, poems, telling of laurel
as symbol of victory, of conquest and the corruption of Empire
exiled because his songs of love and of subtle protest, even as metaphor
anger an Emperor, claiming to be the son of a god, who became a god.
So many tears, so many gods.

Here, in this everyday wood where I walk, the trees are twisted, each
trunk split, hollowed, but growing, not god, not symbol, but trees,
surviving as the old man said, because they are no use to carpenters
nor to gods nor butchers. Though here appears another god, of
eloquence they say, who keeps a company of men, their ears chained
to his tongue. The names trees own are as many as the constellations.

Here in this wee wood, Skeoch, the whitethorn wood, the everyday wood
mocking that god, we took each tree as our alphabet, their secret names
by which we write: *ailm, beith, coll, dair, eadha, uath, iogh, luis,
nuin, ruis, suil*: elm, birch, hazel, oak, aspen, whitethorn, yew, rowan,
ash, elder, willow. Every tree a word, every grove a sentence, every
wood a language. Every man, every woman, every child speaking: a poet.

So many angry, jealous gods. So many tears. So many names.
So many trees. So many poets each singing the breath of the world,
of constellations, transforming anger, jealousy, war into Ovid's love,
the eloquence of trees without chains; the prison of gods.
I write this on Good Friday. *Cedar, pine, cypress.* Another god. Under
every woodland is our origin. Beneath every tree is a door to the Underworld.

walking in, walking on
(900 questions concerning walking)

It's quite clear, axiomatic almost, that to walk in different landscapes is to think different thoughts and thus in different vocabularies and thus also languages. Conasg or conaisg is not the same as whin or furze or gorse, nor yet the same as Ulex europaeus. On the strand, I have no, or few names, for the sea plants that I come across in their reds, ochres, browns and livid greens.

When walking, does one follow a train of thought or a path? Or a Way? Or can it be both?

Is it to follow one's nose or one's feet?

Do we walk the same paths day after day, coming to know the hidden bends, the wayside dockens? Or are they the paths of tradition, those of our forebears, the familiar headlands; Gallows Rock; the wee field known to grandparents as Johnny Mara's? Do we nod in recognition as we pass?

Are we in place?

And what do our bodies tell us? Are we tired after the first mile? After ten miles? And when do we relax into time and place?

And those of us who, for whatever reason, cannot walk, do we walk in our memories or our imaginations?

And when we walk in new places as we sometimes must, do we see the familiar or the novel?

What are our waymarkers: shepherd's purse at our feet or the view between hills?

If we set off at sunrise, do we walk until sunset?

When we walk at night, do we wear dark glasses? Walking nights, do we wear owls?

Is it wet underfoot, or dry, or are we joyous, walking on air? Where is the black dog of despair?

When I walk with another, does my pace quicken or slow?

Do we walk on geology or pavement? Are those the same thing?

Why does that hare cross my path just here? Why does the purple thistle grow?

Why are the greenblue mountains constantly walking?

What are the numbers and names of the bones of the foot?

Is walking a science or an art? Or an alchemy?

Are there walking styles; walking rules?

What are walking aids?

When we walk, do we ride clouds? Are we still when we walk?

Are we walking toward a home we never find? A home we never had?

Is it toes in or toes out?

Is going for a walk the same as walking and if so how?

Sleep walking?

I was out for a walk when I met the shepherd at the top of Carrauntoohill, the highest mountain in Ireland.

Is there walking with purpose? Is it marching? Or is it when I walk to the foreshore to gather kelp or in the woods to gather mushrooms? Is the goose-step fascist walking?

Is marching on a protest demonstration liberal walking? Are dance steps ritualized walking?

When I tore my Achilles tendon in two, I limped for two years. Was I still walking?

Why did Dorothy Wordsworth walk in Scotland? Was it in pursuit of the Romantic or to stretch her legs?

Maighister Alasdair, the father of the great Gaelic poet, a Minister, walked a sixty mile round trip on Sundays from his home in Dalilea to preach in Kilchoan church.

Thoreau had political feet.

Flâneurs may be true Buddhists.

Who are the unsung of walking? Is it quadrupeds or the folk who deliver our post?

Is there such a thing as wild walking, and what would be tamed walking and guerrilla walking?

When the great stag comes down to the glen, is that walking?

When a sign reads Private: No Admittance, do we walk on anyway? Why are certain streets barred to us with large iron gates? Are politicians afraid of walking?

Are we too busy to walk? If so, why do we teach our children to walk?

Why do wood ants walk in single file?

*

My mother always told me I walked at 9 months, so counting on my fingers, I've been walking for seven decades to date. Those of us who can walk are all experts.

Once, as a child, maybe eight years old, I was left behind on the strand where my father had a nut-sweet clinker built dinghy with another man. I was completely forgotten by the men who concentrated on the catch. It was dusk and I thought it was time to set off for the hut. The way was through a wood, inland: this was my first solo walk of some miles and the wood was dark. Because no-one had taught me to be fearful, I was not.

Every walk is a step in the dark.

I lived in Glasgow and worked at the Botanic Gardens there. Every day I walked to work, thinking of plants, of poems. Along the kerbs were masons' marks. The granite of the kerb stones, the limestone paviours, the buildings with their Old Red Devonian ripples of embedded water were my markers and the masons' lettering became my flowers. In this way I walk where no-one has been.

I went to Tibet and walked everywhere at 4,500 metres or higher in thin air. Walking at this height, for me, was unsettling, hallucinogenic. I visited, as a pilgrim, Tsurphu Monastery, then the home of the 14-year-old Gyalwang Karmapa. While waiting for him to receive us all, Tibetans and me, I made a scrambling circumambulation of the monastery, climbing higher than I have ever been, on foot, in my life. Dizzy with fatigue and oxygen shortage, this walk lodged in my feet, my mind and body and remains there still, twenty-five years later. Sometimes a walk has a purpose that is uncertain, even while we think we know what we are walking on, why we are walking. Sometimes the outcome of a walk is very far from what is anticipated. Back in Lhasa, I joined the day-long kora of the Potala palace, walking round, round the exterior walls; one of a crowd of women, men and small Lhasa apso terriers, whose merit on this circumambulation grew with each step – those whose prayers, it's said, are also rooted in their feet, being attached to their minds, driven by their minds.

Back in Scotland, I led a walk round Holy Island, once the dwelling place of St Molaise, whose name, from the 6th century, gives us Lamlash, into which bay of Arran the Holy Island shelters. A day long circumambulation was a time of communal silence. Half way round, though, at the north end of the island, looking up from our feet, began the exclamations of astonishment: an eagle; some seals; the psilocybe mushrooms growing in the dung pats left by the small, wild Eriskay ponies. We walked the paths Vikings would have made through furze and bracken. Our eyes led by our feet, there was no stumbling. Silence. The cries of shearwater and curlew. I carry those silent sounds with me today. It was here I scattered my mother's ashes, here I made kora for lost love, here I celebrated the drawing near of new love, walking on.

Another monastery: Eihei-ji in Fukui Prefecture in Japan. Founded by the philosopher Dogen Eihei who established sitting meditation in Japan after his visit to China in the 13th century. I had been following on foot the long gone trail of the poet Matsuo Basho who passed this way in 1689. Along my route, I had been greeted by an old friend: shepherd's purse, that small and low growing white flowered plant with heart-shaped seed heads as small as the purse of a poor person. No coins ever change hands for these wee tokens of imperishability. Two new friends (for minutes each) had granted me gifts. The first was a man, walking at low water mark (I was at high water mark) near Kanazawa.

We both walked slowly northwards, aware of each other, curious. When we came together, he gave me a single stone, one of a few he had collected, though language difficulties stopped his explanation. The only stone I carried on that walk. I enjoyed his wayfaring, at home here, his dwelling among the stones thrown by the sea, dice of immanence, shared, walking. Like me, he blew his nose into the sea water one nostril at a time. The body ever with us. At the top of a steep hill the orange seller, no-one around for miles, refused my few coins for one of his fruits; placed two oranges and some strawberries into my hands, with no words. Humbled, I passed along the hillside where a raccoon ambled across my path as I sucked an orange, refreshed: my left foot now a sea stone, surfing, surfing, my right foot a sandal of shepherd's purse. At long last near Eihei-ji, wandering the byway, I could not find the monastery, nor understand the directions asked from an old woman selling pestles with stone mortars. Wordlessly, she took my hand as one does a child and led me for half an hour to the monastery gates, bowed and left. My herbs are ground in one of her mortars now. Her kindness balm. How stories create our paths. That sea stone gatherer reminded me of an anecdote in Nyogen Senzaki's collection of ancdotes from the 13th century Sasekishu (Sand and Pebbles) retold by Paul Reps: where a monk is reproved for using tissue to blow his nose: so wasteful of paper; the monastery, of Dogen's mind puzzle: that the bluegreen hills are constantly walking and that in order to live this, not to understand, we must first know our own walking. Which is always someone else's walking as well.

It was halfway through this walk that I sat down on a boulder by the sea for my lunch. A single peanut butter sandwich was all that was to be had in a little wayside store. It was torn from my hand by a small and fast flying kite, stooping on prey like any other raptor, leaving only a bloodied thumb and palm. The walking of a bird. So we bring our own bodies and awareness and memory to bear; that memory which is faulty: was it that walk or another where the kite tore my hand?

On a two month walk through south western US deserts, visiting atomic and nuclear weapons test sites, another stone, or rather atomic-bomb-fused desert sand, was my pocket touch piece: Trinitite, named after the site of the first weapon test site at Trinity New Mexico. Here J Robert Oppenheimer, the conductor of atomic warfare scientists told another story, from the Bhagavad Gita "Now I am become Death, destroyer of Worlds". In his walk Oppenheimer has become multi-armed Vishnu. Trinity itself, in the Jornada del Muerto desert (which might be translated as the day-walk of the dead) is named after John Donne's Holy Sonnet XIV: Batter my heart, three-person'd God… Time in loops, feet in circles, minds in confusion, our gods ever with us. I came eventually to Death Valley, 80 metres below sea level, passing down, then up, on day walks of dissolution.

Walking is repetitive. Sometimes we do forget our own walking but we come to remember it through precisely that repetition. Upwards of 30 years I've walked round here: Cumbrae, Faslane, Carbeth, Glendaruel, a few square miles of woodland, glen and mountain. I step into the names and languages of each place. I note the other inhabitants of my territory, the shepherd's purse, the eagles, mud and the sandy strands. And the stories and the strange occurrences of white harts, of mountains walking alongside me: Dumgoyne, Dumgoyach, Beinn Biuidhe, Auchengaich, Maol an Fheidh, and the razor-fenced nuclear capability of Faslane below Glen Fruin, scene of ancient slaughter; where I walk to protest. Fas lann, meaning an enclosure of wasteland, with its ruined 13th century chapel dedicated to St Michael the Archangel who will "arise at the end time".

I walk my island daily, through inhibiting Estate land then along the long strand to where headland becomes rocks slick with weed, first one way, left foot lower on the camber, then back, right foot lower, and know through my feet I am the true inheritor of this land; me and those like me and before me, who possess land, who, through virtue of walking it, with purpose, dwell here. The gift of a book as a young child had me believe in tracking done on foot, by First Nation north Americans who walked with their toes in line with their heels. White folk, the book informed me, walked with toes pointed out, splay footed. A story I carry on my walks, especially those hirples of two years' standing after my broken Achilles tendon, my walking vulnerability exposed, spirit willing, but flesh weakened.

The philosophy of walks eludes me. There are only individual walks in places made unique each day with each new cloud pattern, each new flowering of season, each washing tide shifting stones, but also literal flowerings, coltsfoot, wood sorrel, broom, and from the dark mycelium underfoot, chanterelles: for me there is just the walking, the process.

To engage with a story, our own stories, is to step into the world as it is. There is no dichotomy between where we walk and how and on what we walk. No culture, no nature. From this place springs all cultures, all of our natures. Basho, at the start of his 1689 walk, heard the singing voices of farmers planting rice: "culture's beginning / from the heart of the country / rice-planting songs". Rice planting is a walk through paddies, a step at a time, while placing seedlings in the wet earth. What Basho heard was humans as part of nature, which is always local, creating a specific of culture. The word translated here as culture is fūryū, literally 'flowing wind', which in Japanese can mean both culture and nature. Little differentiation. Culture in English may mean the ideas and customs of a society as well as to nurture cells for growth. Here we might have the Gaelic dualchas.

So we carry our bodies with us, daily laden with memory, a mental backpack of which the mind-memory (not body-mind-memory) is part; body memory. I once walked across Scotland planting tree seeds as I went. Another time, again across the country, I walked coast to coast for Sense, the charity for deafblind people – 33 miles the first day in rain so unremittingly heavy that towards the end of that day I looked longingly at the cemetery toward the end of the route: how sweet to lie down; but those of us who walk, who cannot but walk, already have a home.

I'm writing this in order to find out what walking is; the names of plants, rocks, birds in the local tongues. I walked round the small island of Cumbrae in a day and wrote a poem: the island in September, which a friend translated into old Scots. My knowledge of the island was broadened by language strata. Does it matter which island if it is a circumambulation – kora – an embodiment of the littoral, a literal rounding of headlands: all muthos become text of my re-marking of territory as in my identity dissolving loss of lover, loss of mother, gaining of blue mountain walking, gaining of love itself: a mild and irreverent humility born of the knowledge and cherishing of evanescence. As ever then, how to know the island, is knowing the stories, the Gaelic of here; but also my own hard won physical knowledge of agriculture, of horticulture's old ways, old footpaths of being.

Each walk is a new story, or a new chapter in a long story; we may limit the walking to one place or include many; these are variations on a theme, these are the narratives we live by, that we jump into, feet first.

A pilgrimage is a walk with a spiritual purpose. Kinhin is a walk with no purpose. A shepherd walks for protective purposes. A boundary walk is a walk with proprietorial purposes. None of these is mutually exclusive.

And the miles I racked up on the farm walking the cows home to the milking parlour, observing the cut-willow fence-stakes root, leaf and grow over the seasons. As a poet it is not purposeful that each instance becomes a poem, if poetry comes from reverie, of bovine rumination; a meditation where the mind is as empty as the habituated walking body is alert.

Walking is dwelling: in common with every species, every living being, we are hefted here on this luminous sphere, since there can be no dwelling without a dwelling place. It is our only dwelling we are walking on.

"And when you change the landscape / is it with bare hands or with gloves?" asked Pablo Neruda. Is it with cars or our feet? With our feet we activate the verbs of the earth.

under the tarmac the garden

buried in ignorance
the sun in darkness
the music of the world is lost
under the hard shield of grief
under the shadow of loss

we have buried the sun
that in season would sprout
plunging hands into soil
rooting into darkness
the broken is mended
we grow in wonder

we are of the soil
fingers deep into rich earth
through barriers
of skin and tissue, bone
raising our mothers'
mothers' earth warmth

kin and custom
this is our home ground
patient, dormant
all that leafs
in the colours of our
fading beautiful bruises

grounded, earthed, rooting
translating radiance
hyssop myrtle basil
nigella marigold
foxglove poppy
snapdragon

flickering
a cosmos of light
eastern bluestar
lambent
in the echo
of memory

landscape now lit
in arcs and crescents
refracting violets
wild indigo
yellow-orange marigold
lupine blue
poppy red

now and here
tentatively in ones and twos
then swarming
the bees will come
the pollinators of our dreams
so the day is made

the corners of the seasons

with a deficit of vision to try to see round the corners of seasons / as if round cornered headlands of an island where all burns must lead to the sea with the bens looking on / since time does not move in a straight line / as the moon does not move in a straight line / the old clock moves showing her face in a circle the hours repeated / returning them never the same

as conifers walk north at one kilometre each year / broadleaves westward at one kilometre every year / so the beech arrived six thousand years ago, then walking northward, an ice age ago / slow migration, sometimes helped along the way / and travelling with it, the mosses, the lichens / spruces climbing the hills into snow twenty five metres a year / each tree aware

as if we are given wee gifts from the hazels / earthworms pulling down maple leaves into dark loam / mycelium bursting into ceps / a quarry as volcanic ash / sedimentary shale bedrock / metamorphic slate shards, weathered Devonian grey fissile / uncountable generations' work of worms to build topsoil for the gifts of wild herbs

as if there was a before or after / no straight line no precedence in a returning curve / as flying north the azure damselfly enters the animism of language bearing lapis lazuli becoming wine-dark, blue-green confusion, becoming grey vegetal green, a neat young girl / cruinneag liath / a 300 million year journey to live for five days / as swarms of beauty / as if lifting a stone, lifting geology for the silent scatterings of ancient tribes of Carboniferous slaters

oh and as though unto the hills / this is our walking through upheaval and trespass to recommence a paradise of water and glacier, quiet and abstract as imagination / teeming with living entities / all lifting blind eyes and seeing eyes / this blue mountain walking, our walking / all things flowing upward

and as if a container for antediluvian dreams and desires / cupped hands for lost Pangaea / rills and canals for flowing Panthalassus becoming Tigris and Euphrates / flagons for melting ice caps / iron beakers for icebergs / baskets for Babylon's wheat and for breads of Persepolis / deep cyan bowls for migrant lemons, bone-white ashets for blood-red pomegranates / walking, walking while staying still

as if the sweet zephyrs of the west and the moist Sirocco from the south, the Harmattan from the east / polar winds from the north / hurricanes and tornadoes / the great storms and surge tsunamis / the watersheds and floodplains / the waters of Zion and the waters of Lethe / nurtured under glass

as, as if in gilding the nettle, smoothing the thorn / moon in a puddle / as if to unbend the corners of seasons, to transcend time, avoid locus / valerian root, opium, the embrace of Morpheus / the rose of Sharon and the Damask rose / balsam, hyssop, juniper and saffron / terebinth and the cedar of Lebanon / mandrake, sweet cicely / tulips from the Taurus mountains / heads filled with dew / / then
                        as if all borrowed / as if all a brief survey of the garden

what breaks

what breaks is light
what bursts is light
what seeds is light
what gives birth is light
what blossoms is light
what travels is light
what unbinds is light
what strikes is light
light is what fruits
light is what breaks hearts
light is what brings forth
light is what sings
light is what lives
light is what lives
light is the hand that loves

light split dew

light rain & light rays from the black centre of this orange hawkbit
slight greys at the periphery are autumn's split light
grainy with reds to come as we stare from here to winter white
straining light between sycamore branches
ungreened with season's thin lit movement

but for now the summer moves sight playfully
into the spectrum of lit hawkbit & the prism of bright
rain revealing a fresh dark stripped of its hold on colour

ripped cloud stirs the day's shadow across the hill's
suite of rowan berry motes dancing red in vision's
slight grip above the lips of countless heather bells
& purpling hips of burnet rose bruising the afternoon
move between what can be seen & what is not there

colour's tripped again tumbling rainlight's play
into summer's intangible trace of rainbows' split white
spilt over green over red over purple over grace over grace

we breathe

we breathe quick
silverly across blue

dogge's mercury
speaking to stones'

plants' constellations
hearing deeper

the many wandering
emissaries of plasma

plant light
each evening

sends morning
benison

notes towards a Pavilion for Listening to Rain

Needs must start at the end.

(Kingdoms / dynasties passed).

It should be told how he died, but later, later, first: the dew.

The order in which things happen, in which they become, is often in doubt (or at any rate, of memory).

Did the Ship's Captain abandon his boat for good before building his house? Or after? It's said that an oak beam from the ship shored up the house front.

Did he plant, as Tiresias instructed, an oar, even though he had sight of the sea and could smell its tang from his house plot?
Was it him or another who planted the roses?

Who watched his house recede, disappear into a faint blue haze of land as they sailed away?

We should now concern ourselves with the middle, where a woman heard a bird sing. Time collapses, the story is told in another tongue.

Shadows, are they all shadows on deck?

Sometimes crickets can be orioles, they sing too.

All day the scent of lilies fills the hall. It is not enough, there must be the songs of orioles, the airs of orioles, the airs must fill the hall. Plant willows by the window, orioles sing in green willows.

Those long summer sermons when dust motes were seen in the air, drifting in sunshafts, falling slowly landing between floorboards. One hundred and sixty three years of dust; the weight of two chaffinches, to be gathered and swept, rising once more into air, ancient dust, clearer than Psalm 103, sung here once.

Is St Jerome's Study a pavilion? In Dürer's woodcut portrayal, made some time five hundred years ago, lion at Jerome's feet, on the wall are implements that can only be for a garden, or possibly metaphor for cutting through metaphysical thickets: billhook, shears, what seems to be a saw blade, and a broom. The study of a study illuminates the notion of all such huts, halls, studies, studios and pavilions as located in entirely rural locations of the imagination, or at the very least where boundaries between town and country are blurred, indistinct.

Today, the street gutters are lined with fallen cherry-blossom petals; the back hill lanes with cuckoo flowers. Who can tell town from country?

Is it not enough that each word in every language is a pavilion?

And what of the ghostly memories, the ghosts of the timbers of this pavilion?

The rain pavilion contains four windows: one to look out over the garden, one to look onto the rock face (within which St Jerome's study is located) another to view a church wall with its buttresses, and the fourth, small, round, a porthole onto the wild, from which we have all come forth and which still remains in us.

And when the winter winds blows, what of the orioles' songs? Here, it rains all year.

What of the bones of orioles, do they become hollow and take flight to the mountain tops and the moon, to sing?

The rain pavilion already existed in the woods, the leaves of the canopy the sounding board.

Rather than steal any tree from the woods, nine pine seeds (an auspicious number) were sown four hundred years ago, with plenty of space in this temperate climate to grow straight and tall. Felled, seasoned and planked, their first thankful task was as floorboards into which dust settled for more than a century and a half, though some were also eaten by worms.

She draws comfort from personal ritual: that she will not pay attention to the oriole's song until she has replaced her morning teacup on the mat after her first delicate sip.

As the first notes of the zither striking up, so, to her, the song of the oriole, calling, calling for a loved one to return.

The rain pavilion sits at the northern end of the dew terrace.

She pauses in the evening, listening to orioles, for some bitter bamboo shoots and bitter tea.

The Pavilion for Listening to Rain may only exist in his imagination. It might change shape and size many times, but its purpose is always clear. Of a painting by Wang Hui, he reads "A lone man sits in a viewing pavilion contemplating the waterfall before him. Mist is forming in the valleys" and wonders what was heard.

The Hall for listening to orioles is made of Manchu yellow pine and laurel. There are two storeys. It sits at the southern slope of Longevity Hill, to the east of the Hall of Dispelling Clouds among the Garden of Clear Ripples, the Hall of Jade Ripples, the Garden of Virtuous Harmony and the Hall of Smiling Pleasure, through the Gate of Inviting the Moon to the Retaining the Goodness Pavilion and the Autumn Water Pavilion.

All night he dreams of orioles, she of soothing rain on the western wind. There is the sound of bells of neighbouring pagodas morning and evening and a cave from which the wind arises.

Five drouthy weeks and nothing but the rasping cough of deer, then, over night, rain.

One hundred and sixty three years ago, the year of the building here in the grounds of which the Rain Pavilion will one day come to be built, the Hall for Listening to Orioles was burned down by invaders. For a decade, the orioles did not sing. The willows grew apace, each spring greener than the last.

Outside the Hall men practice calligraphy with long brushes. They paint only with water, their brushes dipped in the lake, the Garden of Clear Ripples being forbidden them. They paint on stone paving slabs, which, already being geology, become faint and fading poetry; memories of orioles' songs which have pierced them during long spring days.

His eyes as lenses he looks two ways. Inside he sees himself asleep; outside, what he thinks is rain falling on green leaves. He sees all this but recognises nothing.

The smell of the centuries' pine needles is not enough. He must build a Pavilion for Listening to Rain from pines. And again, the scent of roses after rain enchants him still.

Rain is a word. Rain is also a being, in the sense of sentience and a phenomenon, in that it happens. It also happens itself. Sometimes this, sometimes that. When it brings the west wind we call it small, sweet. When it flies in from the east, we cry it bitter. Heidegger probably never listened to rain.

Rain is also a thought, a speculation, an imagining. There is no geometry of rain unless geometry is also defined as absence. In the Rain Pavilion, which is an imagining, a thought pavilion, on the roof he listens to all the rain of the Atlantic falling. He listens fiercely to the rain of the North Sea pounding; the hail of hard rain, the snow-beyond-hearing of soft rain, the dust rain of the Sahel. The rainbow is silent.

The geometry of rain demands that it never be confined; it must flow in its cycles. One hundred and seventy eight years ago, Henry David

Thoreau imagined a triangle of rain, beans and his hoe. If so, then perhaps the A side of his triangle straddles the curve of the world to its furthest horizon. Rain cannot be wrapped.

Do rain gods answer rain dances? Does Zeus dance in lightning? Coyote dances for sure, but the rain bringing nymphs, the Hyades?

Can something six feet square be called a Pavilion? It's not a tent for sure. Maybe it's a hut. It's somewhere lost in the dark shadows cast by Euclid and logical philosophers. The Rain Pavilion in reality fits two people. Vimalakirti's hut, though a hut of ten feet square, was able to accommodate a vast multitude of visitors. In The Hall for Listening to Orioles banquets were held, but there is no record of its size, though once it was trees, then ash, then trees again.

Rain rising is the steam from water and fire together. In the Rain Pavilion is an iron stove, perhaps forged from iron smelted here from charcoal made from felled oaks. On the stove doors are cast flowers dog roses he likes to think, which grow not only on the stove but the edges of pine woods. Pine woods now diminished by four hundred thousand acres.

Manchu yellow pines mostly all cleared by the time of the Hall for Listening to Orioles, but Emperors can be very persuasive.

How is rain measured, he wonders. Is it by the bucketful from the spring well of childhood, or by the months of drought? Do trees make rain? There it is in the end-grain of every timber of the rain pavilion. It is obvious that the saw is conditioned by rain, and what is sawdust but dry rainfall.

Does seeing rainfall make it more beautiful, or hearing a downpour on the tin roof in the dark night? Men climb ladders but never reach the rain clouds, whose very names are poetry: stratus, cirrus, cumulus, and on: stratocumulus, nimbostratus, and cirrostratus. Formal variations.

Even though the rain pavilion is smaller than Kamo no Chomei's ten foot square hut, being only six foot square, like his, the joints of the rain pavilion are held together with metal fastenings. In this case, nuts and bolts reclaimed from someone's abortive attempt to level a floor here; the timbers from the same attempt. The bolts, five, seven and nine inches long jangle together as he tries them out and he is reminded of lightning and storm. He is building in his workshop. The pavilion is like a jigsaw to be fixed, but like Kamo no Chomei's "It would be no trouble at all to take it apart and put it together again". As he works, with augur and bit and saw and setsquare, leaves flutter to the windows of the workshop; herring gulls dance on the old slate roof and he is, for now, happy. But it is for the great clouds he is building, full of water and lightning that refreshes the trees and washes the garden with grace and sometimes lashes with power when it lets down its water, its rain on tree, garden and tin pavilion roof alike. Finished and sitting in the pavilion, listening to the rain, which cleanses and falls on the wise and the fool alike, he will make tea from raindrops and be content to sit with the hound, dry. "Even so, Kasyapa, does the Buddha rise also like a raincloud in this world".

The hound, his friend, drinks long from the tap, which in turn is fed by the rain falling on the long loch here and piped to us. Each single raindrop is larger when sitting in a rain pavilion (so he imagines) as if in a beaten drum; one hears the entire world, on out to the Milky Way.

Each and every puddle here is the temporary resting place of a rain cloud.

A fresh start, since we have foreseen the end of orioles but cannot envisage the end of rain.

Now rainbows are roosting on the pavilion roof.

A humble, narrow door for the pavilion, to respect and welcome the rain, which otherwise must creep in through gaps and crevices, filtered by summer maple leaves and brittle autumn gestures.

The smallest rain is of cloud atoms that bring feathers and omens. He is searching for the lightning knot of the ritual rope that binds the upper and lower estates.

Guillaume Apollinaire, wounded in his temple by shrapnel during the first world war, sometimes wore an iron band round his head. Though it was iron, not tin, Apollinaire danced a poem, calling it a calligramme, which begins "It's raining women's voices".

For the rain pavilion, once in a tin-roofed turf store he had noted that rain has the cadence of voices. A Tang emperor, hearing the rhythm of the oriole's call ordered it to be made into both a dance and a song. Dancing is a form of raining. And ah, the women's voices.

A dancing wave lives in the rain. In the endless cycle from the ocean to the sky, in the wake of geese passing south, the rain hurls. Barnacles fall as hail. What passes for thought is rain.

The Emperor hears rain. Once, when he listened to rain what he was listening to was softly falling melancholy inside his head. He knew that rain, for all his imperial riches, could not buy rain. The sadness coming with the planting of willows, outside the fabled Hall for Listening to Orioles came later, as the Emperor realised he could not order the birds to sing.

In the Hall for Listening to Orioles he built a two storey stage with gilded pillars on which he decreed the sweetest, most enchanting voices of the Opera would sing. And they sang, sweeter to his ear than any wayward golden black-naped bird. He called them orioles. No-one contradicted him. He added this to his Marble Boat and his Bronze Ox, his seventeen arch bridge and his two thousand four hundred foot Long Gallery, built for his mother to observe rain without melancholy or becoming wet.

Who lives between rain and the sound of rain? The gowk. Who wanders with the gowk? The ancestors. How do the ancestors live? Under feathers between raindrops. There are no lost souls. The gowk has volition.

Rain is a chorale. It is after Bach and before Bach, after oriole and before oriole. It's in the pauses, the caesuras, in tears from the twin oceans of samsara and life before life.

Ten thousand years of salt, bitter tears offered to the gods of war, to Mars, to Guan Yu and to Castor and Pollux too, are given back: sweetened, balm of rain.

Warp and weft, he is together with the spider in the rain pavilion. He weaves reverie, the spider spins and weaves reality. Only the rain is truly free.

The oaks, the birches, the chestnuts, the red berried rowans are enchanted by rain. They each sing a lullaby of leaves to passing showers: the lineage of the gods.

Are there tear ducts somewhere that cry this downpour, that swell the apples in this orchard? Rain hisses in the treetops, seethes across the long loch. Who is to say it's not alive?

*

Oh, the rí-rá of rain; the pell-mell helter-skelter of it.

After equinox, after rain is a secondary rainfall. With the winds rising, those small birch leaves shimmy down from their trees, bringing the excess rain with them. Wind's benison.

old invective directive against autumn poems

before leaves fall from the maples make sure your gutters are free of pigeon feathers and summer growth
before the first night frost, split and stack your woodpiles against snow & climate change
before the light fails after solstice lay in a stock of candles in whose light you'll read the old masters
you'll already have salted, pickled and juiced summer's heat
save your seeds in brown paper bags; clean your spade and lean it against the wall
look to your boots, make sure they don't leak; where is your hat?
sweep your path and clear most, but not all, the moss
when you have done these things
write this poem

the deer path to my door

forty years splitting logs for fires eh
cuckoo sings her own name again again

*

easter sunday woken by a bluetit bat
tering trapped in my hut so the days pass

*

mice sleep in the bed when I'm a
way I don't encourage them

*

blackbird & chaffinch sing darkening
day I stare stare mind absent ears

*

arms in rain fetching water from the standpipe standpipe
ing still sky rainbow sheets forming aching forgotten

*

birch & willow herb among roof moss nesting
bluetits in the chimney wall how short my stay here

*

one whole day watched sky
change from grey to blue

*

mushroom days put on dungarees to fix the gutters
at the front today yesterday fixed those at the back

*

buzzard delicately tilting wing tip to tip air
I pour a little water from the bowl overfilled

*

october leaves rivered downstream no fast
er than the empty screwtop wine bottle

*

watched a goosepair become
sky specks dancing eyes

*

evening april snow bonfire rhododendron doesn't
know it's in the wrong place wrong time sorry

*

250 the oak 5 years the apple
planted move in spring winds

*

roof leaks black mould in the corner what
to do plant lavender in a big circle digging now

*

billion volt lightning thunder boomcracks circling
ozone sky smell wet head again what joy what joy

*

in woods bliss is bliss not
ignorance cuckoo's back

*

tomatoes planted out apple blossom
on the bough what have I forgotten

*

cold spuds for lunch as
salt song of the wren

*

weeding such a small hot earth ticks
borrowing my blood

*

hoot & clatter clamour honk disturbed
broody geese I me not needed

*

under the sickle docken rainwet sorrel yellow butter
cups nettle bracken hours brown toad made homeless

*

clegs midges ticks after my blood I'll
never be done with this garden's apples wild sorrel

*

read a page stare at night embers following
thought branch scraping morning roof

*

put on old boots summer meadow walking
sitting goose necks craning

*

move across dream
answering flash of red in the rowan

*

hangover's gone
chanterelles

*

tongue the last wild
strawberry jay's too early for acorns

*

all night roistering wind candle flames
flick is it because I dring too much

*

birch first leaves in the window in
the door in the autumn always astonishing

*

I worry about these apple trees
count branches in the morning

*

what if the path is mud now
wren moves above it

*

between times
an owl shrieks

*

out for a night piss Plough's north out
for another & Plough's east is all

*

the and and and
robin sings

*

old jam
feed the slugs

*

moon & sun together in sky's blue which
is not there where I come from going to

*

autumn behind the apple tree I'm almost not
here the barn owl's screeching

*

quenched candles dying constellation
mice in the oats moonlight

*

raven's pronk talking up sky opens
chest unfastens heart undoes mind sky

*

october hob's yes wheezing kettle
where's the cuckoo now

*

barn owl shrieking tawny owl hoo-
ho-who flyting I keep quiet

*

rains' torrents' soaked pheasants creep low
pause step death comes like that

*

field maple yolk yellow leaves fall on yolk leaves
thoughts drop slowly snowdrops' shoots

*

robin weight twangs snow from rowan twig touch
touch touch I roll barefinger snowballs to throw empty

*

night mountains creaking become white
in morning's mirror me too me too

*

snow so white it's blue
a life of rain sounds become clear

*

which is whiter swans or snowballs
dreep & crackle of ice pretty much I'm idle

*

thoughtless young slaters in the soapdish
shook them outside careless words for

*

roaring high wind
I tilt in my bed good whisky

*

no where when nothing between this
human voice song and canto furling burn

*

two dormant january trees planted
drunk this place drunk avoiding

*

soft owl calls in dawn snow just
so & snow calling dawn owls in

*

sing two birds sing before dawn dark don't
know why I'm awake hear listen world

*

outside night until chill grey
light of no star drink oblivion

*

venus pane by pane through the window
clear as morning's syncopated yaffle

*

moon branches branch shadows
trunks grasses paths can't stop

*

my hope's for the black
slug to safely cross this car tarmac

*

the pond's interior has two herons
inside I swim slow air

*

grub in this oak gall
memory's so short a thing

*

the field maple's topmost branch thrush easily out
sings me

*

neighbour gave me old red brick path
through mud missing deer slots now

*

2 garden bricks here on one the word thistle starworks
on the other robin & I agree there's nothing else

*

two owls & me trade
hoots beyond words

*

wren bides in the bush the crow the oak such
rain something of numbers in the night

*

blossom's on the apple
quince buzz back quick bees

*

it's all blossom now sloe gean lime copper beech
cranefly & me dazed

*

not forgetting the waxing
moon when I sleep

*

gate's made of offcuts fire's made of
scraps wren's thicking her nest

*

cuckoo cuckoos a flittering bat & cuckoo insists
cuckoo all evening long together

*

solid star wheel unsleeping empty blue
bells scent the woods

*

dreams between memory's dreams outhouse sudden morning
    bucks
running teakettle's whistling

*

human I burst from the hut door disturb robin gold
finch blackbird outward off world ripples

*

wren on the doorstep going
out entering depth of spring

*

how I struggle don't struggle colours name form
no form foxgloves campion docken clarity

*

leaves still on the tree wind mooching
as far as they're able I'm rooted here

*

so much sky in this little loch my
ticking idling skull too

*

blackbird's scolding me outside in
side spilt breakfast milk no use

*

crow thinks she's stealing plastic milkbottles from my doorstep
pecking holes & drinking I'm laughing with her

*

aluminium gooseneck
kettle spits steams

*

bank vole's incisors draw down my dropped pasta
wondering how long my teeth'll last

*

I swear the swan's a broken cuckoo
equisetum's up

*

bees
& why is the kettle rocking on the stove top

airs

preludes

WREN

endsong breaking still
it is now
it is only now
it is always now
which is beginning song
world made

*

SPOTTED FLYCATCHER

singer not song
only here here note
now not song now
only singer now not
song now now note
now fly

MISTLE THRUSH

a high clear closure
in throat tuc-tuc-tuc
of smeòrach a psalm

of stormcock a fluting
of wood/wind a lament
a sanctus in livid sky

SONG THRUSH

joy-tongue joy-breath joy-tongue
note against note
for bliss of melody
melody against melody
note onto note
joy-breath air-joy breath-joy

GREAT TIT

a token a counter
there is no time not time
one note two one note two
a heartbeat repeat
sprung rhythm spring
one note no time one note

NUTHATCH

qui-qui-qui who
slant-stone-on-ice song

going up coming down
upside song a ring
downside voice ceòl
a-breath a-voice a-song a-ring

GOLDCREST

first song lost in light
in moss in spidersilk
on woodcock on shortear
on pine in spruce in larch in
larch cedar-cedar-cedar high
sissa-pee herring spink

dawn chorus

(robin, blackbird, herring gull, goldfinch, dove, thrush)

we are walking on emptiness &
light comes from below turning the day
tic   tic-tictsip

tsissip   tseee   tswee
borrowing song &
sound travels on the back of light &
tic   tic-tictsip   tsit
their voices sung   tongues their voices
tswee
a carrying air   a still air

a stilling air   a carried air

bru-dhearg

we tongue their song   we word their tongues

broidileag   *broinnileag*

to give their talking back to the birds

bru-dhearg   *bruin-dearg*

deargan   *nigidh*

oral   oran   spoken sung   &

sometimes a bird   enters the house

tchink tchink tchink   *tchook tsee*

we have heard   she lives in our ears

lón-dubh   *druid-dhubh*   &

she is our woods window

dubhan eun-dubh   *lón-dubh*   *lon*

our ears her note

lon   *lonag*   *lonan*   *londubh*   *lonan*   *lon*

through air   a clear air   a carrying air

kleeuw gah-gah-gah

expelled air   a stilled air   ringing

glas-fhaoileag   *faoileag mhor*

syringeal   tracheal

yeow   *keow*   *kha-ha-ha*   *kha-ha-ha*

wingbursts   of heart & beat

switt-witt   *witt-witt*

first heard with the eyes

lasair choille   *lasair srach*   &

what song is not speech

cantata chorale

coo-cooo   *coo*

calaman   *calaman-coille*
tchuck-tchuck-tchuck   *sip sip*
cearsach   *cullionag*   *smaolach*   *smeol*
a light air   a carrying air
a stilling air   a stilled air
filip filip filip codidio codidio quitquiquit tittit tittit tereret tereret tereret

being time

the sense of the water of the oak
sense of the air in wood
knowledge of the oak in air
knowledge of oak in the wood
sense of knowledge in sense
the crow in the oak

*

song of the thrush
sense of sound on air
knowledge of tree space in thrush-song
thrush weight on the branch
thrush weight on air sense
song weight on air space

*

hearing slow rain in air
sound of air rained on
knowledge of hearing air
edging sense
movement hiss
smack of rain on leaves

*

hinds on the path
    /   no hinds on the path
sense of presence
sense of absence
knowledge of hind space
bracken moving

*

bedrock bulk hill of Dumgoyne
sense of no sky
sky colour in loch water
sense of no colour
water meets air   air meets sky
mute swan

*

digging wet earth under moss
wind moving bracken

no sound of wind
sense of wind
knowledge of hearing

knowledge of no-sound in muscle

guilt is a partial truth

scolded by tree jays
serenaded by sky geese
the morning's poised
a blade's thickness
through pines & oaks
drops of red on forest paths
one day they will come
the stab antlered stags
of cut memory's body
but we slitslip across
the border where
the slice is tender
where the blade is slender
they will come one day
they will come

folly

is this the time for self-reflection
        this is not the time for mirrors

is it possible to let dreams in
        wisdom will tell you no and yes

is wisdom on the other side of folly
        folly is on its own side

where then does wisdom come from
        the fertiliser of wisdom is folly

what is the folly of God
        that We think therefore He exists

then whence our daily bread
        from the baker who counts thirteen as twelve

what then are the follies of the old gods
        that they can transform us into trees

are any of the gods wise
        as wise as fools who make them

does wisdom come with age
        folly would have you believe so

what are the seven ages of mankind
        you must recite folly seven times

then there is no point in any belief
        many follies are believed in

what are the attributes of folly
        plumpness sleekness and glossiness

how may wisdom be acquired
        wisdom is an infection to be avoided

if wisdom infects us how would we know
        how indeed

who will deliver us from folly
        consult Google

ah what are the songs of wisdom
        form follows function

then what are the flowers of wisdom
        stinkhorn and henbane

what are the events of wisdom
        the absence of clouds

what is the silence of wisdom
        our names are strange to us

what then are the events of folly
        the presence of cumulus on the horizon

so what are the rituals of folly
        simplicity duplicity and mockery

and the rituals of wisdom
        as above so below

what can we expect from wisdom
        a child counting stars

and from folly
        a child counting stars

and anything more
        wisdom is its own sinkhole

and what is the word for folly
        shapeshifter

then it is wise to be foolish
        who would know who would know

the grounds

for Paulette Dube

1

no longer a question of what
the language is using us for but who

>	*what is there in those who are?*
>	*that is not hard*
>	*it is who we are not*

in the north woods there when the wind
from the north is there is a cailleach
birch there who groans there

somewhere in this there is a doe screaming
not everything is seen at once

when glas is uttered
can it say wild garlic green

as mac ind Oic's birds of vision and ecstasy
sing themselves to exist and come yes arrive

no longer a question of what
the language is using us for but where

>	*where is there in the cailleach wood?*
>	*that is not hard*
>	*it is the place we are within*

that is that in that there is a wood in
the north which has a word for

oldwomanwhochangedherselfintoahare
in indeterminate pronoun

so we are used here
to become awake here

urgent parliaments and grammars
of woods bird fish deer wolf call

2

-memory of her
-sacred to the memory

-burial place appointed
-as also his relict

-his faithful
-their son departed

-ye ninth day
-in memory

-sincere freind
-who desisted of life

-heir lays the corps
-the buryial place

3

we do not see everything at once
hind leg snared between top strand
and middle strand of barbed wire

wailing fear and agony
my hands torn on barbs wrenching
barbed twists apart from bone

and ligament flesh hanging
whose blood is this on us both
the doe runs free dragging a leg

in that same cailleach wood
eight seasons passing eye to
eye now impaled on doe stare

we stand unblinking minutes
certainty and consanguinity
what there is in those who are

without title
poems for the symbiocene

> there are
> still songs to be sung on the other side
> of mankind
>   —Paul Celan: *Threadsuns*; trans Pierre Joris

there's four wrens to a penny
each wrapped in scraps of sacking
there's ten iterations of this timed existence since
the wren is king of the dog rose and also a sheep
she is an eagle's pinion and a blinded owl
the wren grasps all of time in her beak and space
Ach! Oh! Mother Wren! She is bramble fruit and
thorn wren is bracken spine and frond her troglodyte shell
holds the living world a frightened stone in my hand
wren is the brume that sweeps shadows
she makes bog-myrtle-rips in the silk of dwelling
wren furthers the lyrics of furze her is also trickster Fox
he-at-her heather wren laughs

*

when the alder is a whip it is a cow
when it is felled it becomes two-and-a-half milk cows
alder is not a fern but a fiddle Alder is a Salmon oh
you who have fine fins swim leap redd at my roots
alder sweet is as many eels as they has limbs on her trunk
alder is ladder to the upper sky holes
allis shad and twaite shad vendace and powan

all true black alders when consumed
sparling are lenticels on their alder glutinous twigs
black alder is purple and their sap is hæmoglobin
alder they love them-self and measure corpses
with lichen and cockroaches prophesy the end time

*

no need for sirens the seas sing themselves
no need for Poseidon ocean waves ride themselves
needless Nereus every wave is white haired
no need for Charybdis with sea's maelstrom maws
the Graeae envy every tongue frothing at shores
Proteus unheeded with every heave roll and turmoil
no skin shedder no selkie no sea hog no sea hound
the seas sing and sussurate separate from haaf fish
their own chants and thunders roars and ice-crackings
no plucking gods ocean tsunami to claim lands
how far is the moon sung by sea the wyrds moon this
and the seas mountain themselves rising greendark

*

by its wool a sheep is bracken
with silver mycellium reaching each
fronds uncurling yow lungs
hoggets gimmers taking the earth
fiddleheaded flock spreading
across hills steadily cropping sapiens
each wether a heifer-to-be

*

dear dair oak are two-ten-hundred sibling symbionts
the stone the rock
the rainbow the rain the storm
a wave is also the ocean as an acorn is also/already a boat

*

the whitethorn is a holly imprisoned in a cellar
the cailleach and bodach of the woods're only also two-and-
    a-half milk cows
the apple is unthinkable to destroy
the sentinel pine has a forest held in its roots

*

a heifer becomes blackthorn shedding
horns but always with thorns of the wood
with them sit whitethorn
all milk cows as they become polly

*

fiddlehead bracken is a hogget in
spring they stravaigs the hillside
where they grows hefted spring
ing as the lamb they were for milk

*

rushes asleep are cattle
their breath sweet with pith-milk

and the weight of
light

*

an old tup with curly head is
also bramble ever fruitful the
two are one tangled kin not a lie

*

a wether sings
clear as a bell
as pollard oak
for what is
ever lost

*

& the brown bull
being part wave being
at once all kine

& the red bull
being salmon being apple
pippin codlin pome

& brown & red both
eagles both maggots
whale & seaworm both

*

before they have teeth
alder trees are geese

*

sweetness on the tongue
is already every cherry
of the gean present
in the eye of an incalf cow

*

pin cushion moss rolls
from the woods at night
become tide stranded
medusa

*

the smallest shrew
in winter nest hole
in spring flies out
as wren, king of all birds
no nonsense

*

language stalking
the low hills
become tongues
of whin

*

blood drawn from
a burnet rose
also is a yearling heifer

*

& then the hound for wolves
with its teeth & great size
is wolf & is also at once
butter dough & curds

*

stots being one quarter
butterfly and part curlew
part willow bud
part microbe am
not that old
old yew who told
this story before

*

just for one day
in every year
all lambs are
cuckoos as well
with wings (re
peated) gu-gú

*

her dancing hooves
ten worlds each
inside the innocent
heart of a heifer
hooves the dance
of a field maple
leaf casing

*

all light become flesh
a brindled cow is
dappled shade in wood
land a black coo's
moonlight on the hill
back ways

*

& a dun cow
is quenched flame yet
still burning
these things are so
& a clear eyed bull
calf is naturally a deer
a hind once buck
these things are so

*

& the top third
of each birch tree
is entirely made
of blackbird songs
& those songs
fluting psalms
& those radiant birds
are half bronze
bells of a saint
& but that of
the trees them
selves birch
is as holly

*

what is a split in
a young birch bole
that is easy
the vagina of a hind
from which a calf
is struggling
silvered in caul

& what is the
silver of caul
also easy it is
a shining trail
across worn stone

*

every where again tups'
horns are coiling
round the oaks
of the seaboard's
woods calling them
selves woodbine

*

twin lamb being
sward bouncing
potent tormentil

*

it's the case
that a colt is
part stinkhorn
part stag
part bere
none of these
can be un
woven un
hefted un
hilled

*

besides
an old yow
is the cradle of

a multi stemmed
field maple

*

bay polypore
also being
a mare
with black
hooves

*

as greenblue
hills are only
ever time
ever space
empty underneath

*

as from the empty
hill stone
emerging salmon
waterless
out ranging bull
un pastured

*

sleeping the
dogrose
uttering dreams
of great grand
dam wolf
hound

*

thus raven when
not reflection
is memory
of mammal
of cloud shadow
of bones broken

*

where the moon
light strikes it
is not moon alone
but also hope

*

how many stomachs
is in a small black cow

simple is four stomachs
in a small black cow

stomach of the honeycomb
which is the dance of bees

stomach of the psalter
each leaf a praise

stomach of the harmony
each praise a song

stomach of the savannah
being airs of the ancestors

*

in the same language
the grey mare
& the cockerel both
follow the line
join melodies
in the one salm

*

seals are
certainly people
already walking
on land

*

the mouth of
any salmon
is a constellation
her back
the years

*

dilisk is known
to be triad
part moon yes
but also salt
& barnacle
goose ah
yearling solan

*

yaffle in this airt
is four leaved
birch
whitethorn
sycamore
oak

*

and dolphins
swim among
birches
as hawks

*

it is the law
that bees
are fish

*

every autumn
your vixen
is a red maple
meantime she
is stoat
is lifeblood
is shadow

*

blue mountains
are blue hares
leppin green
are grasses who
lowp white winter
are blaeberry
are wraith

*

the yodel of the herring gull
the speak of the hoodie crow
& twice the call of the tawny owl

these it is known
are the four legs
of a stag in flight

*

a fox glove
too has legs
of a red tailed
bumble bee

*

it is known but
a tick's head
is the left hind leg
of a seven tined stag
while the tongue
of a midge is
the hair of a nettle
that bites

*

this that
one by one
a blue house
fly is silk & lightning
& nine thousand eyes
& the iridescent shade
of a horizoned hill

failing dusk
falling

*

and of the
shit beetle they
are hallowed
dwellers

*

summer hares
become part windrow
part gealt
& bit deer
with leather horns

*

even as they voice
they sandpipers
old blacklips cows dream
of the fledgling they
are which will
not be contained

*

but only the earth
worm wears a saddle

she is made absolutely
of the crackle
of aspen leaves
in west winds

*

buzzard has the ears
of young cats they who
are melancholic
crying for voles they
begin to be

*

slaters being harmony
of the underbelly
of the world
which is stars
which is basalt & roots
chasms & tremor
which is time itself
fourteen legged

*

crottal is a fish
walking above rock

*

and but that green
leaves are also pink
is indisputable
and ripe flesh

*

the ragwort moth
in death besides
is a chaffinch corpse
one same life

*

well
adders
vipers are both
firebolt and wolfs
bane

*

so the sum is
a snuffling hound dog portion
as the brown mushrooms
are the rumblings of oakwoods
so the yellow mushrooms
are the songs of the glades
& the red mushrooms
are the dreams of roe deer

*

& the slug
on the sickener
is half rainwater
half hallucinations

*

the straight grown ash
has no memory of the plank
the one hand span plank
has no memory of the ash
the timber is the tree is
the hand span taken
both living

*

swarming honey
mushrooms
is the dance
of gnats
in shafts of sun

*

ivy ash tree
tawny owl
call all one
diamond mind

*

the unassailable
elder
       trinity
corncrake
nettle

*

there are two moons
this ebb & flow
& one is a hare
leap and wane

*

and oh the third
cry of a raven
is a leaping
deerhound

*

then the smile of a wave
is the grin of a dog

*

madly hound moiety

*

a dog's voice
high above the woods
likewise is a raven

*

well so then
summer sloe and
furze begin to be
fang of a viper

*

the bull
finch turns
to blossom
becomes apple

*

and then ach
fires' flames
becoming stone
among sisters
along the beach
quenched daily
by waves' spume

*

herring become
gulls become
smoke as they fly

*

and that wet
lit creature
morning

*

tree roots all
slow worms

Acknowledgements

Some of these poems have previously appeared in anthologies, journals and publications: 'Antlers of Water': *Writing on the Nature and Environment of Scotland* (Canongate), 'Walking, Landscape and Environment': *Research in Landscape and Environmental Design* (Routledge), 'Songs of Place and Time': *Birdsong and the Dawn Chorus in Natural History and the Arts* (Gaia Project Press / AEN / Bath Spa University) Oystercatcher Press, Galdragon Press, Dockyard Press, Longhouse Publications (Vermont), *Cordite* (Australia), *Dhaka Review* (Bangladesh), *World Poetry* (China), *Molly Bloom, Northwords Now.*

In translation: *Poesía* (Universidad de Carabobo, Venezuela), *Prometeo* (Medellín, Colombia), *Văn Nghệ Quân Đội* (Vietnam).

For the exhibitions: *Airs Phrases and Notes in Neon: The Language of Birds* (National Glass Centre), *Kunstenfestival Watou* (Belgium), *Gwangju Biennale* (South Korea) and for the exhibition publication *Abbas Akhavan study for a garden* (Mount Stuart, Isle of Bute).

My deep gratitude to the editors, translators and curators.